Plains

Laura Pratt

Weigl

Published by Weigl Educational Publishers Limited
6325 10th Street SE
Calgary, Alberta, Canada T2H 2Z9

Website: www.weigl.com
Copyright ©2011 Weigl Educational Publishers Limited

Library and Archives Canada Cataloguing in Publication

Pratt, Laura, 1967-
        Plains / Laura Pratt.
(Canadian ecozones)
Includes index.
Also available in electronic format.
ISBN 978-1-55388-625-9 (bound).--ISBN 978-1-55388-626-6 (pbk.)
        1. Natural history--Boreal Plains Ecozone--Juvenile literature.
2. Natural history--Mixedwood Plains Ecozone (Ont. and Québec)--Juvenile
literature. 3. Ecology--Mixedwood Plains Ecozone (Ont. and Québec)--
Juvenile literature. 4. Ecology--Boreal Plains Ecozone--Juvenile
literature. 5. Occupations--Mixedwood Plains Ecozone (Ont. and Québec)--
Juvenile literature. 6. Occupations--Boreal Plains Ecozone--Juvenile
literature. 7. Boreal Plains Ecozone--Juvenile literature. 8. Mixedwood
Plains Ecozone (Ont. and Québec)--Juvenile literature. I. Title. II. Series:
Canadian ecozones

QH106.P73 2010   j577.0971   C2009-907282-3

Printed in the United States of America in North Mankato, Minnesota
1 2 3 4 5 6 7 8 9 0 14 13 12 11 10

072010
WEP230610

Project Coordinator
Heather Kissock

Designers
Warren Clark, Janine Vangool

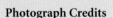
Photograph Credits

Weigl acknowledges Getty Images, Alamy, Corbis, and All Canada Photos as image suppliers for
this title.

Every reasonable effort has been made to trace ownership and to obtain permission to reprint
copyright material. The publishers would be pleased to have any errors or omissions brought
to their attention so that they may be corrected in subsequent printings.

 We acknowledge the financial support of the Government of Canada through the Canada Book
Fund for our publishing activities.

CONTENTS

Introduction

Canada is one of the largest countries in the world and also one of the most diverse. It spans nearly 10 million square kilometres, from the Pacific Ocean in the west to the Atlantic Ocean in the east. Canada's vast landscape features a wide range of geography. Yet, as diverse as the country's geography is, some areas still share common characteristics. These regions are called ecozones. Along with common geographic features, ecozones share similar climates and life forms, such as plants and animals.

Ecozones demonstrate the reliance between **organisms** and their environment. All organisms have unique survival needs. Some organisms thrive in cold, while others require hot climates. They rely on their environment to meet their needs. Just like a puzzle, every organism has its own place in an ecozone.

Canada's plains ecozones possess most of the country's farmland. Many farmers take advantage of the land to grow crops, including canola.

Wetland areas can be found in many plains ecozones.

Canada has both terrestrial, or land-based, and marine, or water-based, ecozones. The terrestrial ecozones can be grouped into five broad categories. These are Arctic, shields, plains, maritimes, and cordilleras.

Within these categories are the five ecozones that fan themselves across the Canadian plains. These are the Taiga Plains, the Boreal Plains, the Hudson Plains, the Mixedwood Plains and the Prairie. Each plains ecozone lays claim to its own particular collection of animal life, plant **species**, natural resources, and human activity. As unique as they are, however, they also share many characteristics.

FASCINATING FACTS

Ecozones can be broken down into smaller areas. An ecoregion is an area within an ecozone that has more precise characteristics than those of the ecozone. Ecodistricts can be found inside ecoregions. These are even smaller areas, with even more in common.

There are different types of plains, including coastal plains and flood plains. Coastal plains rise from sea level until they meet higher landforms such as mountains. Flood plains make up the floor of a river valley beyond the riverbed.

Plains Locations

Plains are broad, mostly flat stretches of land that are lower than the land around them. In Canada, the plains ecozones cover much of central Canada, stretching west to east from British Columbia to Quebec and north into the Northwest Territories. Much of this area is an extension of the Great Plains of North America. This is a large tract of land that stretches south from Canada's North to the state of Texas, in the United States.

Boreal Plains

The Boreal Plains ecozone occupies north-central Alberta, before moving south into central Saskatchewan and southern Manitoba. It also covers part of northeast British Columbia and a portion of the southern Northwest Territories. It is home to a number of **protected areas**, including Wood Buffalo National Park and the Whooping Crane Summer Range.

The Mackenzie River is about 1,800 kilometres long.

Taiga Plains

The Taiga Plains is located north of the Boreal Plains, mostly occupying the southwesterly corner of the Northwest Territories, with small extensions into northern Alberta and northeastern British Columbia. The focal point of this ecozone is the Mackenzie River, Canada's longest river, which thunders through the core of it.

Wood Buffalo National Park is the largest park in Canada and one of the largest parks in the world.

The Mixedwood Plains ecozone has an abundant water supply. This makes the area ideal for farming.

Prairie

The Prairie ecozone is a ribbon of land across the southern parts of Alberta, Manitoba, and Saskatchewan. It features low-lying valleys that contain the majority of the country's most prolific cropland. It is here that much of Canada's food and food exports originate.

The Prairie Provinces are the leading agricultural producers of this country. The climate and natural resources here provide ideal circumstances for growing crops, especially wheat.

Mixedwood Plains

Covering the Lower Great Lakes and St. Lawrence Valley areas, the Mixedwood Plains ecozone is Canada's smallest. Its fertile soils and warm summers make it a productive zone for agriculture.

Hudson Plains

The Hudson Plains runs along the lower portion of Hudson Bay, stretching from Manitoba to Quebec. The terrain is flat and marked by **wetlands** and bogs.

FASCINATING FACTS

The Prairies are called "Canada's breadbasket" because of the abundance of wheat grown there. The province of Saskatchewan alone is responsible for about 60 percent of the country's total wheat production.

The Mixedwood Plains ecozone is the most populated ecozone in the country.

The Great Plains of North America covers about 2.9 million square kilometres of land.

CANADA'S ECOZONES

Canada has five major ecozone categories. Like the plains, however, these categories can be broken down into specific ecozones. The inset map shows where Canada's ecozones are located.

Look closely at the map of the plains ecozones. What features do these ecozones appear to have?

Pacific Maritime

Montane Cordillera

Boreal Cordillera

Taiga Cordillera

Taiga Plains

Boreal Plains

Hudson Plains

Prairie

Taiga Shield

Boreal Shield

Mixedwood Plains

Atlantic Maritime

Southern Arctic

Northern Arctic

Arctic Cordillera

N

UNITED
STATES

Hudson Bay

Churchill River • Churchill

Nelson River • York Factory

Severn River

Manitoba

Winisk River *James Bay*

Quebec

Lake Winnipeg

Lake Winnipegosis

Albany River *Opinaca River*

• Moose Factory

Ontario

• Winnipeg

Moose River

St. Lawrence River and Valley

Red River and Valley

Ottawa River and Valley

Assiniboine River

Georgian Bay • Quebec City

Ottawa • Montreal

Lake Huron

Toronto • *Lake Ontario*

• Niagara Falls

Windsor • Niagara Peninsula

Lake Erie

Plains Features

When glaciers dragged their frozen bulk across this part of the world thousands of years ago, they left a legacy that would define the plains ecozones. Retreating ice flattened the landscape. It also scattered an abundance of glacial deposits in the form of gently rolling plains. Plains ecozones are generally flat in elevation. However, the flatness occurs in stages, with each becoming lower as the plains extend eastward. A variety of other geographic features also define the plains ecozones.

Forests

The northern plains and the Mixedwood Plains ecozones are populated with mixed forests of evergreen and **deciduous** trees. Great clusters of timber cover 84 percent of the Boreal Plains ecozone, and forestry is the primary industry there.

More than 40 different types of grasses can be found at Grasslands National Park.

Grasslands

Grasslands are a type of land characterized by the many grasses that grow there. There are three types of grassland in the plains ecozones: tallgrass prairie, mixed prairie, and short-grass, or fescue, prairie grass. The Prairie ecozone contains Canada's only national park dedicated to the protection of grasslands, Grasslands National Park.

Forests line areas along the Mackenzie River.

Great Bear Lake is 320 kilometres long and about 175 kilometres wide. It is the eighth largest lake in the world.

Rivers and Lakes

Most of the major rivers of the plains ecozones originate in the Rockies. These rivers flow east across the ecozones. They are the product of rainfall, melting snow, and glacial runoff. The Taiga Plains includes most of two great glacial lakes, Great Slave Lake and Great Bear Lake. Great Bear Lake is the largest lake entirely within Canada.

Glacial Deposits

The footprint of the world's various Ice Ages is still visible in the plains ecozones. The deposits left by **glaciation** are now the fertile plains that are responsible for much of the produce Canadians consume. Extensive flat plains of glacial sediment, **glacial kettles**, and **moraines**, are typical here.

Wetlands

Wetlands are an essential part of wildlife **habitat** in the plains ecozones. They often provide refuge for wildlife from forest fires. The Hudson Plains ecozone has the highest concentration of wetlands in the country. Here, the terrain is flat and poorly drained.

FASCINATING FACTS

Scientists have found proof that a large part of southern Alberta and Saskatchewan was an active desert just 200 years ago. It was the result of an extremely severe **drought** that dramatically changed the landscape.

Both the Prairie and Mixedwood Plains ecozones have an **escarpment** as a main feature. The Missouri Coteau is found in the Prairie ecozone, while the Niagara Escarpment is located in the Mixedwood Plains ecozone.

Plains Climate

The plains ecozones have distinct seasons and a wide range of weather. Winters are typically cold, and summers are warm.

Taiga Plains

Due to its northern location, the Taiga Plains experience cooler temperatures than areas to the south. Snow and ice stay on the ground in the Taiga Plains for between six and eight months of the year. The northern reaches of this ecozone experience at least one day when the Sun never rises, and one when it never sets. The annual average temperature in the Taiga Plains varies from –10 degrees Celsius in the north to –1 degrees Celsius in the south. Annual precipitation levels in this ecozone are low, ranging from 200 millimetres in the north to 500 millimetres in the south.

Boreal Plains

In the Boreal Plains ecozone, summers are short and warm, and winters are cold. Average annual temperatures here are around freezing, and precipitation is low. This is because the Rocky Mountains cause a **rain shadow** to occur. This blocks much precipitation from falling on the east side of the mountains. As a result, the ecozone only receives between 300 and 600 millimetres of precipitation each year.

Prairie

The Prairie ecozone is so dry that it is almost like a desert. It is also windy. Summers are short, with limited precipitation, particularly in the dry grassland regions of southwest Saskatchewan and southeast Alberta. Farmers need to **irrigate** their crops for best results here, and frost sometimes destroys them altogether. Winters can be cold, with January temperatures hovering around –25 degrees Celsius. However, winters in this ecozone enjoy occasional relief when a warm **chinook** blows in from the Rockies.

Frost-covered trees are a common sight during Prairie winters.

Hudson Plains

The climate in the Hudson Plains ecozone is influenced by the cold, wet air that lifts off Hudson Bay and the polar air masses that drift over from the north. It is generally cold here. The average daily temperature in January is −19 degrees Celsius. In July, it is between 12 and 16 degrees Celsius. Precipitation in the area is moderate. It ranges from 400 millimetres in the northern part of the ecozone to 800 millimetres in the south.

Mixedwood Plains

Due to its southerly location and the warming influence of the Great Lakes, the Mixedwood Plains has moderate winters. Temperatures average about −5 degrees Celsius. Summers, however, can be hot. The ecozone is prone to violent summer storms, which can sometimes result in tornadoes. There is also plenty of precipitation. It ranges from 750 to 1,000 millimetres per year.

The cold winds of the Hudson Plains can cause trees to have branches on one side only. These trees are called flag trees.

FASCINATING FACTS

Summer thunderstorms in the Plains ecozones are often severe. South-central Alberta has a reputation for occupying one of the worst hailstorm belts in North America.

The Fighting Prairie Weather Dogs is a group of extreme weather fans who chase storms across the Prairie Provinces as a hobby. They provide storm reports to local weather centres.

Scientists claim that the Prairie ecozone will feel the effects of climate change over the next few years. Experts' long-term forecasts predict warmer, wetter conditions for much of the Prairies.

Toronto's CN Tower receives an average of 75 lightning strikes per year.

Technology on the Plains

About 67.5 million hectares of land in Canada is used for farming. Most of Canada's farms are situated in one of two areas—the Prairie ecozone or the Mixedwood Plains ecozone. Both areas have the conditions needed for specific types of farming. In the Mixedwood Plains ecozone, conditions are excellent for dairy farming. The key element to successful farming in the Prairie ecozone is the quality of the land. This is why the Prairies are known for their grain farms.

Soil quality is important to growing crops. Scientists are constantly working to discover ways to improve soil fertility and water quality. They use technology to predict crop production and to control weeds. Local farmers also use tools to improve land quality.

By studying and experimenting with different types of soil, scientists have been able to develop fertilizers that improve growing conditions. Fertilizers have been developed for all kinds of soils. They add nutrients that stimulate plant growth. The quality of a crop can improve greatly when the soil is fertilized properly.

Farmers use scientific advances in agriculture to improve the quality of their crops.

Irrigation is useful to farmers when rainfall is minimal. It allows them to keep the land moist so that crops have good growing conditions.

Developments in soil science have led to the creation of new irrigation methods. Scientists have analyzed the size of water drops and the amount of water different crops need. From their research, they have created ways of protecting the crops being grown while supplying the soil with the moisture it needs.

Different methods of irrigation are now used to water various types of crops. In drip irrigation, plastic pipes with holes in them are laid along rows of fruit and vegetable crops. Water is pumped through the pipes to water the plants. For high-pressure spray irrigation, often used on grain crops, a long tube carries water from a pump. A triangular frame holds the tube and moves in a circle around the pump. The pump sends water to sprinklers along the tube. In low-energy spray irrigation, a large pipe carries water from a pump to small water sprayers that sit close to the ground. The water is sprayed gently onto the crops through the sprayer's nozzle.

FASCINATING FACTS

In nature, it can take 3,000 to 12,000 years for a productive layer of topsoil to develop. Ineffective farming practices can ruin this layer in a matter of years during a devastating drought.

Low-energy spray irrigation is gradually replacing high-pressure irrigation.

LIFE ON THE PLAINS

The plains ecozones play host to an array of organisms that make their home among the many natural resources of the region.

The prairie rattlesnake is the only venomous snake found in the Prairie provinces.

REPTILES

Reptile species are more numerous in the Prairie ecozone than in any other plains ecozone. Here, the relative warmth and dry air suit a reptile's physical needs. Fourteen different species of reptiles make their home here. Most of them live in the region's mixed grassland. It is easiest to spot them when the Sun is high in the sky. Reptiles need the Sun's rays to raise their body temperature. The prairie rattlesnake is one of the best-known reptiles in the Prairie ecozone.

BIRDS

The skies of the plains are filled with birds, including the bald eagle and osprey. The variety of environmental conditions here, from grasslands to forests, provide habitat for a range of species. Some birds stay in the area all year round. Others use it for breeding or when migrating south in autumn. Some birds, such as the ferruginous hawk, build their nests on the ground. The red-tailed hawk seeks out trees for its nest. In winter, snow buntings feed on the seeds and grasses that poke out from the snow.

The Blackfoot people call the snow bunting *aapinakoisisttsii*. This means "little morning birds."

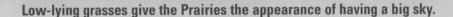

Low-lying grasses give the Prairies the appearance of having a big sky.

PLANTS

Vegetation of all kinds is common in the plains ecozones. In the Prairie ecozone, grasslands are most common. However, plains ecozones also feature many kinds of trees. Trees are more abundant in the east than the west. The Hudson Plains has mainly **coniferous** forests. Deciduous forests make up most of the Mixedwood Plains.

AMPHIBIANS

Amphibians must keep their skin moist to survive, and most need to lay their eggs in water. They seek out habitats where this is possible. In the plains ecozones, amphibians are found in the wetlands and in and around the many water bodies glaciers have created over time. There are several amphibious species on the plains. Among them are the northern leopard frog, the great plains toad, and the tiger salamander.

INVERTEBRATES

Invertebrates are organisms without backbones. They can be found in most parts of the world. Many invertebrate species can be found in the plains ecozones. Here, they are often counted among the most troublesome residents. The grasshopper and flea beetle are two of the most unpopular invertebrates on the plains. This is because of the damage they can cause to crops.

Flea beetles damage crops by chewing small holes in the leaves of the plants.

Plains Plants

Trees

Trees are found throughout the plains ecozones. The majority of trees in the northern plains ecozones are coniferous, while trees in the southern ecozones tend to be a combination of coniferous and deciduous. Coniferous trees common to the plains ecozones include the black spruce, lodgepole pine, balsam fir, jack pine, and tamarack. Deciduous trees found in the southern parts of the plains ecozones include the white birch, trembling aspen, and balsam poplar. Nearly half of the Boreal Plains ecozone is covered with forests.

The prickly pear cactus blooms in the spring. Its flowers can be red, purple, or yellow.

Bushes and shrubs

In the summer, the plains ecozones bloom with clusters of flowering shrubs and bushes. Bushes and shrubs flourish in the Taiga Plains ecozone. Labrador tea, leatherleaf, gooseberry, and blueberry are among the most common. Lying low on the ground, lichens and mosses are like a lush, thick rug. Cacti grow in the driest parts of the plains ecozones.

The white birch is also called the paper birch. This is because of its paper-like bark.

Fescue grass can be found in Cypress Hills Interprovincial Park, on the Alberta-Saskatchewan border. Protecting this grass is a priority for the park staff.

Grasses

While all plains ecozones have grass, the Prairie ecozone is best known for its grasslands. Three types of grasslands can be found here. The short-grass prairies are home to ankle-high grasses, such as blue grama and buffalo grass. June grass and western wheatgrass are just two of the grasses found on the mixed-grass prairies. The tall-grass prairies feature grasses such as big bluestem and switchgrass. These grasses are well suited to the region's harsh climate because of their deep roots. Grasses can have up to 5 kilometres of roots and root hairs. The roots and root hairs allow the grasses to remain firmly attached to the ground when grazing animals, such as cattle, tug on them.

FASCINATING FACTS

In a typical year, more than 1 million hectares of vegetation burn in the plains ecozones due to forest and grass fires. Great effort goes into putting these fires out, but it is not unusual for huge areas of plantlife to be destroyed by a fire.

Early settlers would put the leaves of Labrador tea in their closets to keep away moths.

Birds, Mammals, and Fish

Birds

There are 462 known species of birds in Canada. Many of them spend time in the plains ecozones. Grassland birds include the horned lark and chestnut-collared longspur. Where prairie meets forest, the vesper sparrow and sharp-tailed grouse nest. The forests are also home to the red-headed woodpecker and western meadowlark. In the wetlands, plains **waterfowl** make their nests in the spring and raise their young in the summer. Among them are the common loon and Canada goose. The whooping crane, perhaps Canada's best-known **endangered** species, nests in the wetlands of Wood Buffalo National Park. Many birds of prey live in the plains ecozones. Birds of prey are birds that hunt other animals using their keen senses, sharp talons, and powerful beaks. Owls and hawks are common birds of prey here.

The yellow perch is a freshwater fish. It is found in lakes and rivers across Canada.

Fish

The lakes and streams of the plains ecozones teem with fish. The northern pike and carp are **predatory** fish. They hunt lake whitefish, yellow perch, and lake chub. Some plains water bodies are crowded with fish not native to the region. These fish were introduced to the waters when inland shipping routes were developed. Lampreys are the most well-known such fish in the Great Lakes. They feed on indigenous species. In some cases, this has led to the decline of indigenous species, such as lake trout, in the Mixedwood Plains ecozone.

When defending its territory, the chestnut-collared larkspur flies into the air, spreads its tail, and sings as it dives downward.

A coyote can run at speeds up to 64 kilometres per hour.

Mammals

One way to categorize the mammals of the plains ecozones is according to what they eat. Animals that eat meat are called carnivores. Carnivores in the plains ecozones include the coyote, black bear, muskrat, river otter, lynx, badger, and wolf. Coyotes eat mostly rodents, which are plentiful in plains ecozones, along with some birds and insects. The badger favours ground squirrels, which it catches by digging. Squirrels are herbivores. These are animals that eat only vegetation. Other plains herbivores include elk, moose, and pronghorn antelope. The pronghorn antelope is thought to be the world's second-fastest land animal, after the cheetah. Scientists believe the pronghorn antelope developed great speed in response to the need for it to outrun much faster predators that are now **extinct.**

FASCINATING FACTS

If there was a mammal mascot to the Prairies, it would be the bison. The bison is the largest land mammal in North America. A bison can weigh as much as 900 kilograms and stand as tall as 1.8 metres. In the early 1800s, millions of bison roamed the continent, but overhunting cut their numbers to hundreds. As well, when early settlers arrived in Canada, 87 percent of Canadian grasslands was used for agriculture. The bison lost much of its home.

More than half of all the ducks in North America are born in the plains wetlands.

Beaver and muskrat pelts have an insulating layer that makes them warm. Early settlers hunted beaver almost to extinction for their warm furs.

Invertebrates, Reptiles, and Amphibians

Earthworms can grow to be almost 2.5 metres long.

Invertebrates

Many invertebrates live in the plains ecozones. Each contributes to its **ecosystem** in some way. Some invertebrates serve as food sources for other animals. Other insects and bacteria serve the ecosystem as **decomposers**. Earthworms, for example, are important grassland invertebrates for the work they do in maintaining soil. These useful plains residents eat decaying plant and animal matter and then return its nutrient-rich components to the soil.

Reptiles

The prairie skink is a small lizard that prefers not to show itself. It only comes into sight in the spring, when it breeds in the grasslands. Like other snakes, the common garter is not capable of long migrations, so it **hibernates** through the winter in the southern plains ecozones. There are only two venomous snakes found in the plains ecozones. The massassauga rattlesnake is found in the Mixedwood Plains ecozone, and the prairie rattlesnake is found in the southern part of the Prairie ecozone.

The common garter snake has the widest distribution of any snake in North America.

Wood frogs can grow to be about 8 centimetres in length.

Amphibians

Amphibians can be found inside those parts of the plains ecozones that are naturally damp enough to sustain them. The wood frog often breeds in temporary water pools. Scientists believe it does this in order to avoid natural predators that live in permanent water bodies.

FASCINATING FACTS

The massassauga rattlesnake is threatened in Canada. Its population has declined mainly because of habitat destruction.

The great plains toad is found throughout southern Alberta and southwest Saskatchewan. When threatened, this type of toad inflates itself, lowers its head, and extends all four legs in a defensive posture.

Plains Animals in Danger

As human settlement and development increased on the plains, the environment and the animals that rely on it changed. This is especially true in the Prairie and Boreal Plains ecozones. These two regions are known as the most altered parts of Canada. Logging, land-clearing, hunting, and pollution have destroyed the habitats of many animals that are native to these regions. As a result, several indigenous plains animals, such as the grizzly bear, whooping crane, and wood bison, are in danger.

Two hundred years ago, between 30 million and 70 million bison roamed North America. They provided food, clothing, and even shelter to the area's First Nations. With the arrival of European settlers, however, the bison became overhunted, and its numbers were greatly reduced. By the late 1800s, the bison was facing extinction. In order to save this animal, the government developed rules that limited bison hunting. It also created a **preserve** for bison to occupy where hunting was not allowed. This preserve was called Wood Buffalo National Park. Since the early 1900s, the wood bison population has been on the rise. In 1988, the Canadian government changed the wood bison's conservation status from "endangered" to "threatened" to indicate that the population had grown.

Today, there are about 5,600 wood bison living in Wood Buffalo National Park.

White-tailed deer can leap up to 9 metres in a single bound.

Other animals have not fared as well as the bison. The plains grizzly bear, for example, has been extinct since the early 1900s. The greater prairie chicken once occupied large stretches of grassland, but when its home was converted for farming and cattle grazing, it disappeared.

Much effort has been made in recent years to protect endangered and threatened wildlife in the Boreal Plains and Prairie ecozones. Federal and provincial governments have created sanctuaries and banned commercial hunting of certain animals. In turn, the numbers of white-tailed deer, elk, beaver, and pronghorned antelope have all increased.

FASCINATING FACTS

The swift fox was extinct in Canada until a program to bring it back was developed in Saskatchewan and Alberta. For 14 years starting in 1983, the provinces reintroduced 900 swift foxes into nature. Though most died, enough survived to produce a small and promising swift fox population in the area.

The Whooping Crane Summer Range, in the boreal forests of northern Alberta and southwestern Northwest Territories, is the world's only nesting and breeding area for the endangered whooping crane.

Canada removed the peregrine falcon from its list of endangered species in 1999, improving the bird's status to "threatened." Some people call the reintroduction of the peregrine into nature one of humankind's most impressive environmental successes.

WORKING ON THE PLAINS

The people who work with the land, plants, and animals of the plains ecozones need to have a strong understanding of the factors that affect the area. The fires, nutrients, climate, and everyday happenings on the plains are of great importance to farmers, field biologists, and soil scientists.

FARMER

- Duties: raise crops and tend land

- Education: Formal education is not critical for this profession, but some farmers earn degrees in agriculture or in business with a concentration in agriculture

- Interests: agriculture, animal science, the outdoors, physical activity

Farmers manage their own farms or work for other farmers. They determine the best time to plant seed, apply fertilizer and chemicals, and harvest and market their crops. Farmers need managerial skills to operate a business. A basic knowledge of accounting and bookkeeping is important. Computer skills are also increasingly necessary. Farmers must be prepared to work long hours and to abide by the inconsistencies of the weather.

FIELD RESEARCH BIOLOGIST

- Duties: studies animal habits and habitats

- Education: bachelor of science in wildlife management, master of science in natural resource management

- Interests: wildlife, habitats

Field research biologists explore and monitor animals in their environment. Field researchers sometimes trap certain species of animals and release them in places that have smaller populations. This allows the population to grow.

SOIL SCIENTIST

- Duties: studies soils and the implications of soil use

- Education: bachelor's, master's, or doctoral degree in science, Earth science, or a related discipline

- Interests: the environment, microbiology, math, chemistry, geology

Soil scientists investigate soil conditions to determine the biological, physical, and chemical activity taking place in the soil. They can then provide advice on how to restore damaged land and how to maintain these conditions. Soil scientists use their keen problem-solving skills to analyze information and interpret scientific results.

ECO CHALLENGE

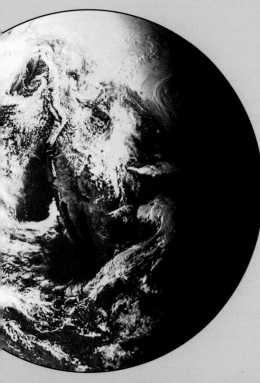

1 Name two types of plains.

2 Why are the plains called "Canada's breadbasket"?

3 What is the claim to fame of Grasslands National Park?

4 What is a chinook?

5 Name three types of irrigation.

6 In what part of a plains ecozone do amphibians normally live?

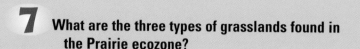

7 What are the three types of grasslands found in the Prairie ecozone?

8 What is the largest land mammal in North America?

9 How many venomous snakes are found in the plains ecozones?

10 Which two plains ecozones are known as the most altered ecozones in Canada?

Answers

1. Coastal plains and flood plains
2. Because of the wheat that is grown there
3. It is Canada's only national park dedicated to the protection of grasslands.
4. A dry wind that occurs in the shelter of a mountain range
5. Drip irrigation, high-pressure spray irrigation, low-energy spray irrigation
6. In the wetlands of the ecozone
7. Short grass, tall grass, and fescue grass
8. The bison
9. Two
10. The Boreal Plains and Prairie ecozones

CREATE A GRASSLAND

To stimulate a patch of grassland, try growing wheat grass in your home or classroom.

MATERIALS

- Paper towel
- Water
- Wheat grass seeds
- Bowl
- Potting soil
- 2 seed trays
- Plastic grassland animals

 Mould may grow between the blades of grass. Do not eat the wheat grass.

1. Moisten paper towel with water. Place wheat grass seeds on the paper towel.

2. Place the moistened paper towel and the seeds in the bowl. Let them sit for 6 to 12 hours or until they sprout.

3. Place potting soil in seed trays. Put the sprouted wheat grass seeds in the trays. Cover with more soil. Moisten with water.

4. Watch your wheat grass grow, adding water when needed.

FURTHER RESEARCH

How can I find more information about Canada's ecozones, the plains, and animals?

- The Internet offers an abundance of information on all of these topics.

- Libraries have many interesting books about the plains and the organisms that make their home there.

- Science centres are filled with information about what life in Canada's plains ecozones is all about.

BOOKS

Bradley, Catherine. *Life in the Plains: Animals, People, Plants.* Two-can Books, 1997.

Donaldson, Chelsea. *Canada's Prairie Animals.* Scholastic, 2007.

Watson, Galadriel. *The Interior Plains.* Weigl Educational Publishers Limited, 2006.

WEBSITES

Where can I learn about plains plants and animals?

Canadian Biodiversity
http://canadianbiodiversity.mcgill.ca/english/ecozones/prairies/prairies.htm

Where can I learn more about Canadian agriculture?

Agriculture and Agri-Food Canada
www.agr.gc.ca

Where can I learn about endangered species?

Nature Canada
www.naturecanada.ca

GLOSSARY

chinook: a dry wind that occurs in the shelter of a mountain range

coniferous: a cone-bearing tree

deciduous: trees that lose their leaves for part of the year

decomposers: organisms that feed on and break down animal and plant matter

drought: an extended period of time during which a geographic area experiences a deficiency in water

ecosystem: a community of living things sharing an environment

endangered: a species threatened with imminent extinction

escarpment: a long, steep slope separating two areas of different elevations

extinct: no longer in existence

glacial kettles: shallow, sediment-filled water bodies formed by retreating glaciers

glaciation: the formation of glaciers

habitat: an environment where a plant or animal makes its home

hibernates: passes the winter in an inactive state

irrigate: to deliver water to a dry area

moraines: accumulations of glacial soil and rock

organisms: living things

predatory: preying upon other organisms for survival

preserve: land set aside for the protection of animals or natural resources

protected areas: places that enjoy certain governmental protection because of their environmental value

rain shadow: an area having relatively little precipitation due to the effect of a barrier, such as a mountain range

species: types of organisms that share specific features

topsoil: the upper layer of soil

waterfowl: birds that frequent water

wetlands: land areas that are waterlogged for all or much of the year

INDEX